Where I Live:
Coming Home to the Southern Mountains

poems by

Jennie Boyd Bull

Finishing Line Press
Georgetown, Kentucky

Where I Live:
Coming Home to the Southern Mountains

I dedicate these poems to my spiritual teacher,
whose love and grace sustain my heart.

ACKNOWLEDGMENTS

I'm grateful for the support of three writing and critique groups in the
South Toe River Valley—Eve's Night Out, Poets Under the Maples, and the
Breezeway Writers. In particular, Marilyn McVicker, Kathy Weisfeld, Anne
and Sam Maren-Hogan, Cathy Sky, Mendy Knott, Joann Hodshon, and Britt
Kaufmann offered gentle, wise critique of these poems over my first year in
the valley and continue to encourage me in my work. I'm also grateful for the
Great Smokies Writing Program memoir course taught by Catherine Reid in
2016, which inspired me to venture from private to public with my work. And
to friends Anita McCurley, Sandra Bromble, and Patricia Bernarding, whose
hospitality and generosity fostered my homecoming.

Publisher: Leah Maines
Editor: Christen Kincaid
Cover Art: Alice Aldrich
Author Photo: Alice Aldrich
Cover Design: Ranice Crosby

Printed in the USA on acid-free paper.
Order online: www.finishinglinepress.com
also available on amazon.com

Author inquiries and mail orders:
Finishing Line Press
P. O. Box 1626
Georgetown, Kentucky 40324
U. S. A.

Table of Contents

Prologue Weave

Table of Contents

Prologue Weave

I choose to weave the later years of my life in the South Toe River Valley, deep in the mountains of Western North Carolina, in a 750-square foot house by a stream, with goats next door. Tomatoes and basil grow out back. Two little neighbor girls knock on my door many afternoons and ask me to push them high in the swing hung by two strong ropes from a pine tree in my front yard.

A simple, two-harness table loom sits on the counter, patiently waiting for me to learn to weave. Neighbors offer their hands and gifts: Jane lends the loom; Nanci repairs it; Joyce brings a basket of yarns, tools, "how to" books; Patti teaches me to create the steady tension of warp—measure the ends, sley the reed, thread the heddles, tie evenly to the back beam. I barter with handfuls of tomatoes.

Intertwined with these new skills and vocabulary is the mystery of flow. These warp threads form the constants on which I weave the weft of my life—spirit, body, community—in a rhythm of patterns and colors breathing in and out, up and down, to create a whole fabric of use and beauty. May I weave such intricate balance in my new life here.

This valley breathes out, growing green produce and fruitful children who nourish the wider earth. The valley breathes in, gleaning artists and retirees to amend the soil for next year's garden. I am a layer of compost, here to weave my future in this fertile valley. Yet, the steady warp threads of these mountains and their watersheds continue to define this rich land, inspiring and enlivening its people with their beauty, fertility, and diversity, for those who live with eyes, hearts and minds open to the wisdom of earth and sky. I marvel—write poems of discovery this first year.

Discovering Where I Live

Where I Live

The street sign announces Passional Way,
        just after Powderhorn and Pinwheel.
Jenna, Milly, Evie, and baby Bibi live just down the hill.
Goats live next door.

The postal address is Burnsville, North Carolina.
The map location is off 19E on 80 South.
The realtor listing is Blue Rock area.
The voter registration is Micaville Elementary.
Friends say South Toe and Celo.
When I give directions, it's between Bowditch Union Church
        and Poplar Grove store.

It's a little, green, pointy-roof house along a country road
winding through the tallest mountains in the East.

Florence's husband helped build it.
Jane's husband used it as a jewelry studio.
Sarah's husband installed the electricity at renovation.

I sit on the swing in the yard, under pine, chestnut and pear trees,
        to sing and watch the chickadees and chipmunks play.
I practice tai chi with soft pine needles under my feet.

Lily the cat and I live here—we call it home.

Crest Trail

I hike along the summits of these towering, ancient mountains—
      historic Mitchell, Craig, Big Tom,
      Balsam Cone, Cattail Peak, Potato Hill,
Then steeply down to Deep Gap;
      leave Winterstar, Gibbs and Celo Knob for another day.

Up I puff,
      down I clamber
On miles of rocky, leaf-covered trail,
      in the crisp, blue morning air,
Ancient mountains of fiery color
      spread below me.

Along the crest of this glory
      I watch each step,
      alert to the ground before me.
Rock and Sky
      Earth and Heaven
         joined in each breath.

Tomatoes

With the advice of Dig In! community gardeners, I prepare a lasagna bed:
  layers of cardboard, grass clippings, manure, straw, mulch
  at the end of the gravel drive,
  a sunny spot with stream nearby,
  perfect for my first garden.

I plant beets seeds early this spring,
  add tomato starts in sturdy plastic containers at one end;
  but the seeds are too old to sprout—
  tomatoes soon take over, with sprigs of basil.

Now it's late September—I harvest
  sun golds, tommy toes, big cosmonauts,
  ever-spreading ground cherries.

Sold to me as tomatillos, the aptly named ground cherries,
  diminutive, sweet, pale yellow tomatoes with papery husks,
  sprawl all over the bed, into the grass,
  over the gravel pile by the driveway.

The tommy toes grow fast and tall—
  they topple one of the tomato cages,
  tendrils wander onto the grass,
  hide the container.
  Dig In gardeners say they are "indeterminate;"
  even with suckering, as I've been taught, they continue to expand.

Every morning I visit the garden to harvest ripe tomatoes,
  stuff my pockets, hoodie, bag, pot, or whatever is handy,
  peer under the thick leaves and vines,
  search for glimpses of bright red fruit;
  then crouch down on hands and knees,

stretch to gather the ground cherries littering the earth,
husk lanterns ripening from green to brown.

Carrying my load into the house,
I dump them all in the sink to wash,
begin sorting ripe from unripe,
whole from split,
insect-nibbled from intact.

Ripe tomatoes go in the fridge in recycled plastic yogurt containers,
sorted by kind;
still-green go on the window sill in plastic lids to ripen;
the split, I pop in my mouth.

I crank the food mill to make tomato puree,
stash jars in the freezer along with bags of whole tomatoes,
plop tommy toes in my salad for lunch every day,
garnish potluck dishes with yellow ground cherries,
blend a huge bowl of gazpacho for my study group,
give every friend who drops by a handful,
especially the little girls next door.
I barter with tomatoes.

Assorted containers overflow in the fridge and on the counter—
more ripen daily;
I'm in lush red and yellow tomato heaven.

Snow Melt

I'm from "off," a renter, new to the valley.

Since summer, I've nested in this mountain community,
    joining up, reaching out, getting to know the place,
Grateful for the kindness and generosity of friends and folks I've met
    in the South Toe Valley.

And yet, near neighbors maintain a frozen, distant silence:
    the young mother down the hill never speaks,
        but waves as she drives by.
    the retired realtor next door tells me over the fence
        he doesn't want his goats
            eating the multiflora rose along my backyard stream.
    the woman who lives across the road is never out of the house.

Now it's winter—a snowstorm is coming.

I gather my courage, walk across the road to visit the old woman
    as she unloads groceries from the car into her wheelchair cart,
    ask if I can park my car along the road below her trailer,
    the one covered with a big blue tarp.
"Yes, honey, I know what it's like," she says—
    offers me her driveway too.
My heart warm with relief and her kindness,
    I vow to help her when I can.

The snow falls and falls and falls—
    I measure twelve inches by the bird feeder,
        where I watch and watch and watch the cardinals and juncos play.
On the third day, I trudge up the snow-covered drive—
    dig out my car along the road.

I remember my neighbor and her girls down the hill,
      marooned by the steep, drifted drive.
      I text, "I'm out—can I bring y'all anything?"
The next morning, she texts to thank me,
      says it's been six days since she's been to work,
      she's asked a man to come plow the drive for $150!

I email the landlord—
      "clearing the drive is in the rental maintenance agreement;
      my neighbor needs to get to work—can you clear it soon?"
By 9 a.m. the next morning, three men with shovels begin at the top and
      work their way down for hours, clearing the drive;
      together, the neighbor and I finish shoveling at the bottom;
      we talk parking strategies, glad not to pay the $150.
We're neighbors.

Snow softens in the sun,
      near neighbors thaw,
         the ice is broken.

Coming Out at Book Group

Last month, one of the women assumed I'm straight.
      As a single, older woman, I resolve to correct the image—
      North Carolina passed anti-gay legislation, my rights are at risk.
This month, we discuss a novel exploring homophobia in a mountain town.
I note the power and subtlety of the treatment,
      then come out—
"I am a lesbian, have worked for years in the lesbian and gay community."

      Silence in the room.

The discussion continues.

      My heart races.
      Blood rushes to my head.

Later, one woman redirects the discussion to politics.
Another smiles, winks at me as she speaks.
As people leave, I am alone.
After all these years being out, I still feel the risks—
      exposed,
      rejected,
      excluded.

Am I risking other people and groups?
Am I safe in this group?
Is it helpful?

I write this poem.

Doctrine of Discovery

As a woman raised white, Christian, descendant of
        an Englishman who "owned" the Carolinas,
        whose family enslaved African peoples as commodities,
        I come home to my past.

I come home to the Carolinas of the present—
        the horror of a Black pastor and worshippers
        murdered as they pray at Bible study,
        the amazing grace of our President's healing words.

I drive long hours to a family reunion
        at a beachfront home near Charleston,
        to hear my uncle brag he has "no Indian blood."
        Where am I? Who am I?

We are European Christians, so we can rule and convert the world,
said the Pope and the Monarchs. We—
        launch Crusades to save the infidels from themselves,
        grant the Carolinas to Englishmen to pay off our debts,
        divide up Asian countries following our wars.
To this day, the legal code of the United States cites the "law of discovery"
        to deny Native American property rights and reparations.
Appropriation is the word—if the Europeans come, they own it,
        dehumanize the earth and its peoples wherever they go.

"They" is me—an arrow in my heart.

I resolve to use awareness of privilege to right the wrongs,
        open to discover kinship, kindness toward all beings.

I promulgate my heart's doctrine of discovery—
        seek connectedness,
        listen with humility,
        act in community.

Workin' on the Building

for Lesley Riddle

In Burnsville Town Center at RiddleFest, thirty voices rise in song.
A Jubilee Choir of mostly Scotch-Irish and a few Black faces celebrates
      the African-American tradition of open-hearted praise,
      filled with sorrow, longing, faith, determination,
      "workin' on the building" of our lives in community.
Together in praise,
      we honor the gifts of Black music to mountain music—
      from the heart.
A mountain town center filled with remembrance, unity, pride.

Windfall

Two old trees stand tall in the yard,
      leafless branches heavy with pear.
Green mottled windfall litters the grass below,
      hiding russet wounds, the feast of beetles.

I hear the soft thump of falling fruit.
Neighbor Sarah and the Internet inform me
      pears are ripe when still hard but easily plucked.
With this cold snap, now is the time.

In the chill evening light, I harvest the windfall,
      unlikely treasure to put by for winter.
I glean the pears, excise the wounds, store them
      to cook with oatmeal on winter mornings.

Bowls, baskets, bags of speckled fruit dominate the kitchen—
      sweet abundance to be shared, relished, buttered, preserved.
Wounded fruit,
      the gift of aging trees.

Where I Live Inside

Tai Chi

The body flows
    softly
        gently
            easefully

With the pulse of the breath,
    gathering inward,
        expanding outward,
            in the circle of life.

Yin and Yang,
    stillness and movement,
        beginning and ending with nothing—*wu*,
            in the middle, everything—*tai*.

The mind moves in focused stillness with the pulse,
    led by body's memory of legs, torso, arms,
        chi flowing up from the earth to the *tantien*—
        red field below the navel,
        up the spine, out the hands, eyes, top of head.

I am whole,
    beautiful,
        powerful,
            surrendered,
                aware.

Still like a mountain,
    flowing like a river,
        I play tai chi.

Heartseed

The seed of my heart
Is a blackened, cracked husk
Through which light pours,
      sweet birdsong pulses,
      purple flowers dance.

From that center,
      soft green ferns
              unfurl,
Offering shy smiles
      to moonbeams.

My tender heart blossoms.

Good Company

Soft snow enfolds my world,
rainbows dance along walls,
cardinals flash in snow,
playful juncos peck.

Delicate paperwhites tall in a china pot,
interviews, sonatas, ragas in the air,
soup, greens, cornbread on the stove,
emails, a good book, journaling, poetry,
the flow of tai chi with rug turned back.

Lily the cat perches at the window—
        raccoon tail twitches.
She leaps into my lap,
        soft white underbelly splayed open in enviable ease,
        a warm body tucks against my chest.

Night

Owl hoots in the forest.
Wind roars through the trees,
surges over the mountains,
   recedes to a whisper,
  surges again.

I lie cocooned in my bed;
  the wind breathes me.

Seasons of Meditation

Winter

As meditation descends,
      the crunching footsteps of the mind
      are softly covered in the deepening stillness
      of perfect whiteness,
Leaving faint traces of the path taken,
      blue shadows cast by the subtle light of grace.

Spring

The sap rises,
   pushes through the frozen earth,
   up, up, up the trunk,
   softens, expands,
To emerge as pale green buds of love,
Leafing into ever-new remembrance of life.

Summer

Crickets' thrum pulses with the breath,
Playful birdsong praises the light,
Cloudburst blesses the abundance—
                              sacred green earth.

Autumn

Serenely, like a leaf,
     the mind drops
          into a pool of silence
             and dissolves there,
Grateful to return to its source.

Winter Solstice

Reminders of light shimmer
     in meditation,
     in dreams.

Music stirs sweet memories,
     Lily curls, purrs in my lap,
     my body flows in tai chi.

The laughing stream plays behind the house,
     chickadees peck, flit about the feeder,
     snow swirls, clearing the path,
     trees cast long shadows across mountains,
     stars and planets glitter in expanse of night.

Smiles—kindness of strangers and friends—
     welcome email,
     website photo,
     teaching story,
     bedtime reading,
     music making—"How can I keep from singing?"

Most of all, in the silence—
     wherever it emerges

In that silence is remembrance.

Remember to be still,
                    be silent.

All is part of me.

Jennie Boyd Bull retired to the mountains of Western North Carolina at age seventy, following careers as an editor at the National Trust for Historic Preservation, pastor with Metropolitan Community Church of Baltimore, manager of the 31st Street Women's Bookstore, librarian with Baltimore County Public Libraries, and editor, archivist, and department head with the SYDA Foundation in New York State. She received a BA in English Literature from Swarthmore College in 1967 and an M.Div. from Wesley Theological Seminary in 1982. In 1992, she received the Passages Community Service Award for 20 years of service in the Baltimore and Washington lesbian communities.

Raised in Knoxville, TN, Jennie is grateful to return home to the Appalachians, where she volunteers with the Carolina Mountains Literary Festival, Dig In! Community Garden, and NC High Peaks Trails Association. A Tai Chi instructor, she teaches Qigong and Tai Chi classes in the South Toe River Valley and in nearby Asheville. Her poetry has been published in *Palm of Your Hand, Poetry by Baltimore Lesbians; ENO*, literary arts magazine of Duke University's Nicholas School of the Environment; and *WNC Woman*. She is currently writing a memoir and learning to weave, when she's not swinging in the front yard, weeding the garden, or curled up reading with Lily the cat.

www.ingramcontent.com/pod-product-compliance
Lightning Source LLC
LaVergne TN
LVHW021125080426
835510LV00021B/3325